Concord Theatricals Acting Edition

We Aren't Kids Anymore

by Drew Gasparini

Featuring a Poem by Keith White

CONCORD
THEATRICALS

Copyright © 2020 by Drew Gasparini
All Rights Reserved

WE AREN'T KIDS ANYMORE is fully protected under the copyright laws of the United States of America, the British Commonwealth, including Canada, and all member countries of the Berne Convention for the Protection of Literary and Artistic Works, the Universal Copyright Convention, and/or the World Trade Organization conforming to the Agreement on Trade Related Aspects of Intellectual Property Rights. All rights, including professional and amateur stage productions, recitation, lecturing, public reading, motion picture, radio broadcasting, television and the rights of translation into foreign languages are strictly reserved.

ISBN 978-0-573-70907-4

www.concordtheatricals.com
www.concordtheatricals.co.uk

FOR PRODUCTION ENQUIRIES

UNITED STATES AND CANADA
info@concordtheatricals.com
1-866-979-0447

UNITED KINGDOM AND EUROPE
licensing@concordtheatricals.co.uk
020-7054-7200

Each title is subject to availability from Concord Theatricals Corp., depending upon country of performance. Please be aware that *WE AREN'T KIDS ANYMORE* may not be licensed by Concord Theatricals Corp. in your territory. Professional and amateur producers should contact the nearest Concord Theatricals Corp. office or licensing partner to verify availability.

CAUTION: Professional and amateur producers are hereby warned that *WE AREN'T KIDS ANYMORE* is subject to a licensing fee. The purchase, renting, lending or use of this book does not constitute a license to perform this title(s), which license must be obtained from Concord Theatricals Corp. prior to any performance. Performance of this title(s) without a license is a violation of federal law and may subject the producer and/or presenter or such performances to civil penalties. A licensing fee must be paid whether the title(s) is presented for charity or gain and whether or not admission is charged. Professional/Stock licensing fees are quoted upon application to Concord Theatricals Corp.

This work is published by Concord Theatricals Corp.

No one shall make any changes in this title(s) for the purpose of production. No part of this book may be reproduced, stored in a retrieval system, or transmitted in any form, by any means, now known or yet to be invented, including mechanical, electronic, photocopying, recording, videotaping, or otherwise, without the prior written permission of the publisher. No one shall upload this title(s), or part of this title(s), to any social media websites.

For all enquiries regarding motion picture, television, and other media rights, please contact Concord Theatricals Corp.

MUSIC USE NOTE

Licensees are solely responsible for obtaining formal written permission from copyright owners to use copyrighted music in the performance of this play and are strongly cautioned to do so. If no such permission is obtained by the licensee, then the licensee must use only original music that the licensee owns and controls. Licensees are solely responsible and liable for all music clearances and shall indemnify the copyright owners of the play(s) and their licensing agent, Concord Theatricals Corp., against any costs, expenses, losses and liabilities arising from the use of music by licensees. Please contact the appropriate music licensing authority in your territory for the rights to any incidental music.

IMPORTANT BILLING AND CREDIT REQUIREMENTS

If you have obtained performance rights to this title, please refer to your licensing agreement for important billing and credit requirements.

WE AREN'T KIDS ANYMORE was developed by Drew Gasparini in collaboration with Justin Goldner, Erica Rotstein, and Ilana Ransom Toeplitz, with financial support from Bobbie Theodore and Jana Shea. The original studio cast recording features:

BONNIE.................................Bonnie Milligan
COLTON......................................Colton Ryan
LILLI... Lilli Cooper
NICK..............................Nicholas Christopher
RAY..Raymond J. Lee

WE AREN'T KIDS ANYMORE was first produced by Christopher Newport University at the Ferguson Center for the Arts (Executive Director, Bruce Bronstein) in a workshop production directed and choreographed by Ilana Ransom Toeplitz, with music supervision by Justin Goldner, music direction by Colin Ruffer, lighting design by Andrew Griffin, and stage management by Kyle Ronyecs. The company also included CNU students Benjamin Long (assistant director), Abigail Rozmajzl (assistant music director), and Madeleine Witmer (assistant choreographer). The cast was as follows:

BONNIE.................................. Amara Breisch
COLTON...................................... Elijah Selby
LILLI..................................... Autumn Plucker
NICK..................................... Matt Stevenson
RAY.. Ben Atkinson
ENSEMBLE......................Chris Chapin, Jack Little,
Noah Long, Katie Murphy,
Tanner Payne, Madison Raef,
Remy Thompson, Peyton Townsend,
Madeleine Witmer

CHARACTERS

It should be acknowledged that the names of the characters don't define any aspect of "type." These stories can be told by anyone as long as they connect to the material, so you are encouraged to cast this show as diversely as possible, showcasing performers of varying race, gender, ability, shape, and size. Representation is something we, as artists, must be working toward. Additionally, in order for each character to stand out as an individual, please strive to cast performers who each possess unique qualities.

BONNIE – Vocally, Bonnie is a powerhouse. Someone who can take a soft-spoken sentiment and turn it into an anthem that brings the house down. Each of Bonnie's songs are quite rangy in the sense that they live in a conversational part of the voice until the hook comes around, then *blast off*!

As written: Pop belt-mix up to E5

COLTON – Vocally, Colton should be able to accomplish a folky, storytelling type of tone with some pop sensibility. Colton tells stories about family, which calls for several reflective moments. Colton is not shy, but they are certainly an observer of the past and the present.

As written: Pop belt-mix up to A4

LILLI – Vocally, Lilli lives in the worlds of pop/rock and musical theatre. There is a calmness to Lilli that is exemplified within their songs. Lilli is a little more aware and has accepted more of what is out of their control than the other members of The Group.

As written: Pop belt-mix up to Eb5

NICK – Vocally, Nick should be quite multifaceted. Needing to bring a sultry jazz tone to "I Wish I Never Met You," more of a power gospel tone to "I'll Stick Around," and still be able to hop into the pop/rock and musical theatre styles of the group numbers. The most subdued. The most surprising.

As written: Pop belt-mix up to A4

RAY – Ray has the most ups and downs, and their songs create quite a personal journey. Vocally, Ray, like Nick, should be multifaceted. Able to bring warmth to the ballads, but also able to bring an anger and growl to songs like "I'm Not Falling For That."
As written: Pop belt-mix up to A4

FROM THE AUTHOR

To everyone who has the bravery, the vulnerability, and the empathy to mount this show...thank you. From the bottom of my heart, thank you. I wrote these songs never thinking they could stretch any further than the borders of my comfort zone. Before it became *We Aren't Kids Anymore*, this project started as a musical journal entry that I was keeping for myself. A way for me to express how I was feeling during the space between huge chapters of growth in my young-adult life. As I slowly started sharing this material with others, it didn't take long to notice that there was a lot of adhesive tissue connecting my experiences with others'. No matter how old we are, or how evolved we think we are, we all face a certain inevitability: growing up.

My hope is that each staging of *We Aren't Kids Anymore* is less a representation of what *my* interpretations of the songs are, and more a representation of *your* interpretations. From the sadness that we face through heartbreak, trying to grasp the unattainable, or trying to control the uncontrollable, to the joys that family, success, and reaching for the seemingly impossible might bring us. There is something with which everyone can connect. Again, at least that's my hope.

Theatre is where we are allowed to be the most honest, the most courageous, the most wounded, the biggest or the smallest versions of ourselves. *Musical* theatre heightens those parts of the journey. Through these songs, may you all acknowledge something about yourselves that you already knew and – even more exciting – may you all discover something about yourselves that you didn't already know.

Wishing you all the best with your production of *We Aren't Kids Anymore*, and the artist journey on which you will continue to tell your stories.

Much love,
Drew Gasparini
Composer/Lyricist

ORIGINATING DIRECTOR'S NOTE
From Ilana Ransom Toeplitz

I'm touched that you read the director's note, because I usually skip them. But Drew and I wanted to offer what we hope is a helpful blueprint as you build your own production of *We Aren't Kids Anymore*.

We originally staged this show with a minimal set of five chairs, which were eventually flipped, stacked, and turned as they morphed into skyscrapers, a brunch table in New York City, or a snowbank on Park and 88th.

This musical song cycle was created with the flexibility to be performed by a cast of five principals (Bonnie, Colton, Nick, Lilli, and Ray). There's also the option of adding an ensemble of any size, from five to five hundred players. As a result, we are referring to the cast as an inclusionary "The Group" for the purposes of this libretto.

There are five individual character arcs for a director to track and foster in addition to the larger, collective arc of The Group. After we've established and cracked open the principals a bit, we earn the opportunity for more ensemble-driven storytelling somewhere around "The Thing I Like The Most About New York." In the workshop, soloists used other actors as scene partners to up the ante, tell the story, and give us new visuals – but you should do whatever you want to do to tell the story.

Regardless of your cast size, maintaining an initial sense of anonymity among the five principals is paramount; any scene partners should feel like faceless people in a memory. We must believe that the five named characters are meeting for the first time ever, today.

The dots we use to connect The Group are the breaks between song sections, with static silence and Nick's struggle to speak. Silence is one of your most powerful tools in any musical, but especially this one; I encourage you to use every second of uncomfortable mute toward telling this story.

The point is: less is more, this is a musical and not a concert, silence is golden, chairs are fun – and clear the path for the songs to do their work.

I'm wishing you the best as you explore, shape, build, and put your own thumbprints on your production of *We Aren't Kids Anymore*.

Ilana Ransom Toeplitz

(Lights up on five strangers: "THE GROUP" [suggested seating order from stage right to stage left: RAY, BONNIE, COLTON, NICK, and LILLI] sitting in a semi-circle, facing inward. They sit in mutual, uncomfortable silence. They look at each other. They fidget. They shift in their chairs. There is a feeling of isolation and disconnect among them.)

(We are at an anonymous meeting for addicts; it shouldn't feel too specific. It's ten minutes past the meeting time, and there's no group leader to be seen; they're presumably on a bender somewhere. COLTON taps his foot in tempo to the beat of:)

[MUSIC NO. 01 "HELLO MY NAME IS DREW..."]

COLTON.
HELLO, MY NAME IS DREW AND I'M AN ARTIST.

BONNIE, LILLI, NICK & RAY. Hi Drew.

(COLTON steps forward as if speaking directly to the audience.)

COLTON.
I WANNA KNOW IF YOU WOULD LISTEN TO MY MUSIC.
I'VE BEEN WORKING SO DAMN HARD
ON WRITING SOMETHING WORTH A DAMN.

(COLTON continues to "speak." Mouthing words and gesticulating.)

(LILLI steps forward as if speaking directly to the audience.)

LILLI.
>HI, MY NAME IS DREW.
>SOMETIMES I WISH THAT I WAS
>SLIGHTLY MORE THAN HUMAN.
>I'VE BEEN WORKING SO DAMN HARD
>TO LIVE A LIFE THAT'S WORTH A DAMN.
>
>>*(**LILLI** continues to "speak." Mouthing words and gesticulating.)*
>>
>>*(**RAY** steps forward as if speaking directly to the audience.)*

RAY.
>HELLO MY NAME IS DREW.
>I MIGHT BE CRAZY FOR THIS DREAM THAT I'M PURSUING.
>BUT HERE'S A PINCH OF WHAT A BROODING, BLEEDING
>   HEART MIGHT HAVE TO SAY...
>
>>*(Lights up on **THE GROUP**. Each one representing an extension of "Drew.")*

BONNIE, COLTON & NICK.
>RIGHT THIS WAY.

LILLI & RAY.
>IF LIFE WAS ALL ABOUT THE FUN SIDE,
>IF LIFE WAS ONLY ALL ABOUT THE UPSIDE,
>THEN WE MIGHT NEVER SEE ALL WE SHOULD SEE.

BONNIE & NICK.
>IF LIFE WAS ALL ABOUT THE UPSIDE,
>AVOIDING EVERY CHANCE TO TAKE A NOSEDIVE,

COLTON.
>THEN YOU WON'T SEE THE WRECKAGE
>FROM THE GREATEST PART OF ME.

BONNIE.
>YOU MAY NOT BELIEVE IT,
>BUT SOMETHING GOT ME OFF MY ASS TODAY.

NICK.
>YOU MAY NEVER SEE IT,
>BUT BEHIND CLOSED DOORS
>THERE'S SO MUCH MORE TO ME.

COLTON.
>HELLO MY NAME IS DREW!

>*(Introducing themselves to each other:)*

RAY. John.

LILLI. Hannah.

NICK. Leo.

BONNIE. Susan.

COLTON.
>SOMETIMES I DON'T KNOW
>WHAT THE HELL I SHOULD BE DOING.

BONNIE.
>I'VE BEEN WORKING SO DAMN LONG
>ON FINDING SOMETHING WORTH A DAMN.

RAY.
>MAKING SOMETHING NEW,
>WE ALL LEAN ON BOOZE AND DRUGS.

BONNIE.
>AND MASTURBATION.

LILLI.
>WE ALL LEARN BY SCREWING UP
>AND LETTING DOWN THE ONES WHO STAY.

THE GROUP.
>AREN'T WE ALL CLICHÉS?!

RAY & LILLI.	**COLTON, BONNIE & NICK.**
IF LIFE WAS ALL ABOUT THE FUN SIDE,	IF LIFE WAS ALL ABOUT THE UPSIDE,
IF LIFE WAS ONLY ALL ABOUT THE UPSIDE,	IF LIFE WAS ALL ABOUT THE UPSIDE,
THEN WE MIGHT NEVER SEE ALL WE SHOULD SEE.	OOH
IF LIFE WAS ALL ABOUT THE UPSIDE,	IF LIFE WAS ALL ABOUT THE UPSIDE,
AVOIDING EVERY CHANCE TO TAKE A NOSEDIVE,	IF LIFE –
	AVOIDING EVERY NOSEDIVE...

RAY & LILLI.
>THEN YOU WON'T SEE THE WRECKAGE

THE GROUP.
>FROM THE GREATEST PARTS OF ME.

BONNIE.
>I SMILE TOO MUCH.

NICK.
>I CRY TOO MUCH.

COLTON.
>I LAUGH AT INAPPROPRIATE TIMES.

LILLI.
>I SHARE TOO MUCH.

RAY.
>I CARE TOO MUCH.

BONNIE.
>I NEVER GIVE ENOUGH OF MY TIME.

THE GROUP.
>I SMOKE TOO MUCH,
>I DRINK TOO MUCH,
>I JOKE TOO MUCH
>AND I THINK TOO MUCH.

NICK.
>NO ONE'S PERFECT,
>BUT WHO WANTS TO BE?

COLTON.
>YOU MAY NOT BELIEVE IT
>BUT SOMETHING GOT ME OFF MY ASS TODAY.

COLTON & LILLI.
>YOU MAY NEVER SEE IT,

LILLI.
>BUT BEHIND CLOSED DOORS
>THERE'S SO MUCH MORE.

RAY, NICK & BONNIE.
>HELLO, MY NAME IS DREW!

COLTON. Josh!

LILLI. Tori!

NICK. Stuart!

RAY, NICK & BONNIE.
>I WANNA KNOW IF YOU WOULD LISTEN TO MY MUSIC.
>I'VE BEEN WORKING SO DAMN HARD ON WRITING
>>SOMETHING

RAY.
>WORTH A DAMN.

LILLI & COLTON.	**BONNIE, RAY & NICK.**
HELLO, MY NAME IS DREW	IF LIFE WAS ALL ABOUT THE UPSIDE,

LILLI & COLTON.
  I WANT TO KNOW IF YOU WOULD LISTEN TO MY MUSIC.

BONNIE, RAY & NICK.
  IF LIFE WAS ALL ABOUT THE JOYRIDE,

LILLI & COLTON.
  I'VE BEEN WORKING SO DAMN HARD

THE GROUP.
  ON WRITING SOMETHING WORTH A DAMN.

> *(Focus to **BONNIE**. She is left alone onstage. Like a deer in headlights.)*

[MUSIC NO. 02 "ON THE EDGE"]

BONNIE.
  NOTHING'S GONNA STOP ME
  FROM DOING SOMETHING STUPID AS HELL AGAIN
  IT'S AS IF NOBODY TAUGHT ME
  TO THINK BEFORE I ACT
  WELL WHO'S GOT TIME FOR THAT?
  NEVER NEEDED ANYONE'S PERMISSION
  TO DO ANYTHING IT TAKES, YEAH.
  NEVER NEEDED ANYONE'S OPINION
  ABOUT HOW I LEARN BY MAKING
  TOO MANY MISTAKES.

  I THINK I THINK TOO MUCH.
  I THINK I'M LIVING ON THE BRINK TOO MUCH.
  I'M GETTING READY TO BE TRIPPED,
  I SKIP A STEP,
  I'M TIPPING OVER
  AND I'M HANGING ON THE LEDGE
  I'M SURE I DRINK TOO MUCH.
  MAYBE I DON'T LISTEN TO MY SHRINK, MAN,

BONNIE.
  I'M GETTING SO DAMN TIRED
  OF LIVING ON THE EDGE

THE GROUP.
  AH
  HA HA HA HA HA HA

OF WHERE I'M SUPPOSED TO BE.	HA HA HA HA HA HA
I'M LIVING ON THE EDGE	HA HA HA
OF WHERE I'M SUPPOSED TO BE.	HA HA HA HA HA HA

BONNIE.

AT TWENTY-NINE I FELT THE HIGHEST.
I FINALLY SAW THE CHECKS START COMING IN.
AND SURE, HE MIGHT BE BIASED,
BUT MY DAD WAS PROUD AS HELL
AND ALWAYS LOUD AS HELL ABOUT IT.
NEVER NEEDED ANYONE TO HELP ME
BOY OH BOY, AREN'T I FULL OF SHIT?
I NEVER NEEDED ANYONE TO TELL ME.
TO KEEP GOING
'CAUSE I THINK I KNOW
WHEN I SHOULD QUIT.

I THINK I THINK TOO MUCH.
I THINK I'M LIVING ON THE BRINK TOO MUCH.
I'M GETTING READY TO BE TRIPPED,
I SKIP A STEP,
I'M TIPPING OVER

BONNIE.	**THE GROUP.**
AND I'M HANGING ON THE LEDGE.	AH
I'M SURE I DRINK TOO MUCH.	
MAYBE I DON'T LISTEN TO MY SHRINK, MAN,	HAH
I'M GETTING SO DAMN TIRED.	
TIME STANDS STILL.	
THAT'S WHEN ENERGY'S REQUIRED,	
	AH
WHEN TIME STANDS STILL,	
AND I'M GETTING SO DAMN TIRED.	AH

BONNIE.

NEVER NEEDED ANYONE'S PERMISSION
TO DO ANYTHING IT TAKES, YEAH
NEVER NEEDED ANYONE'S OPINION

BONNIE.
>ABOUT HOW I LEARN BY MAKING
>TOO MANY MISTAKES.

	THE GROUP.
BONNIE.	HAH
I THINK I THINK TOO MUCH.	
I THINK I'M LIVING ON THE BRINK TOO MUCH.	
I'M GETTING READY TO BE TRIPPED,	
I SKIP A STEP,	
I'M TIPPING OVER	
AND I'M HANING ON THE LEDGE.	HAH
I'M SURE I DRINK TOO MUCH.	
MAYBE I DON'T LISTEN TO MY SHRINK, MAN,	HAH
I'M GETTING SO DAMN TIRED	HAH
OF LIVING ON THE EDGE	
	HA HA HA
OF WHERE I'M SUPPOSED TO BE.	HA HA HA
	HA HA HA
I'M LIVING ON THE EDGE	HA HA HA
	HA HA HA
OF WHERE I'M SUPPOSED TO BE.	HA HA HA
	HA HA HA
OF WHERE I'M SUPPOSED TO BE.	

>*(BONNIE exits as COLTON enters. They do not see or acknowledge each other.)*

[MUSIC NO. 03 "DANNY AND ANDREW"]

COLTON. *(As a toddler.)*
>GOOD MORNING, DANNY.
>NICE TO SEE YOU, DANNY.
>HERE WE ARE THIS MORNING
>AT THE TOILET CROSSING STREAMS.
>MOM GOT OUT THE RICE KRISPIES,
>I KNOW THAT THEY'RE YOUR FAVORITE.
>AND THAT'S WHY THEY'RE MY FAVORITE.

'CAUSE DANNY, YOU'RE MY FAVORITE,
YOU'RE MY BIG BROTHER.

DID YOU HEAR, DANNY?
IS IT TRUE, DANNY?
MOM IS GETTING FAT
BECAUSE SHE'S PREGNANT WITH A BABY,
WHICH MEANS JUST LIKE YOU
I'LL BE A BIG BROTHER TOO.
BUT I LEARNED FROM THE BEST,
YOU'RE MY BIG BROTHER.

I GET EXCITED
WHEN YOU ASK ME TO HANG OUT
WITH ALL YOUR OLDER FRIENDS.
WHEN YOU DO,
I GET EXCITED YOU'RE EXCITED THAT I'M THERE.
WE'RE A PAIR,
DANNY AND ANDREW.

(As a young boy.)

OKAY, DANNY.
I'LL DO, DANNY.
I'M NOT SURE HOW THIS IS FUNNY,
BUT YOU'RE LAUGHING
SO I'M LAUGHING.
IF YOU'RE LAUGHING, THEN IT'S FUNNY,
AND WE'RE LAUGHING SO IT'S COOL.
SO I'LL DO IT 'CAUSE YOU'RE COOL.
EVERYTHING YOU DO IS COOL,
YOU'RE MY BIG BROTHER.

IS IT BAD, DANNY?
KASIE'S MAD, DANNY,
'CAUSE WE SCRAPED HER BARBIE'S BOOBS OFF
ON THE CONCRETE IN THE DRIVEWAY
SHE'S THROWING A FIT
AND WE'RE IN DEEP SHIT.
BUT IT'S WORTH IT

COLTON.
>'CAUSE I'M HANGING WITH MY BIG BROTHER.
>I GET EXCITED
>WHEN YOU ASK ME TO PRANK
>OUR LITTLE SISTERS, 'CAUSE IT'S FUN
>WHEN YOU DO.
>I GET EXCITED YOU'RE EXCITED THAT I'M THERE.
>WE'RE A PAIR,
>DANNY AND ANDREW.
>
>*(As a pre-teen.)*
>
>I HAD A CRUSH ON *ALEX MACK*
>AFTER YOU EXPLAINED TO ME
>THAT SHE WAS PROBABLY
>THE HOTTEST GIRL ON TV.
>WE ALWAYS SEEM TO AGREE ON THINGS LIKE THAT.
>
>*(As a high-schooler.)*
>
>WHAT'S UP, BROTHER?
>HOW'S COLLEGE, BROTHER?
>I'M THRILLED TO HEAR
>THAT YOU ARE COMING BACK TO VISIT.
>THE GIRL YOU'VE HAD A CRUSH ON
>HAS BEEN ASKING HOW YOU'VE BEEN,
>AND SHE'D LOVE TO GET TO SEE YOU.
>BUT DON'T FORGET TO MAKE TIME
>FOR YOUR LITTLE BROTHER.
>I GET EXCITED
>WHEN YOU TALK ABOUT THE FRIENDS YOU'VE MADE
>SINCE YOU MOVED AWAY
>JUST LIKE YOU,
>I FOUND MY CALLING BUT IT'S ON THE OTHER COAST.
>BICOASTAL BROS, DANNY AND ANDREW.

(As a young man.)
HEY, DANNY.
HOW'S THE FAMILY, DANNY?
THINGS ARE PRETTY BUSY,
HARD TO FIND THE TIME TO TALK.
CONGRATS ON ALL YOU'RE DOING.
HOW IS MY LITTLE NEPHEW?
I CAN'T BELIEVE HE'S TURNING THREE.
I'VE NEVER BEEN SO PROUD TO BE
YOUR BROTHER.

> (**COLTON** *exits.* **LILLI** *enters. They do not see or acknowledge each other.*)
> **[MUSIC NO. 04 "TURN THE PAGE"]**

LILLI.

MAYBE I'M NOT EXACTLY WHERE I THOUGHT I'D BE.
MAYBE I'M FORCED TO REDEFINE REALITY.
MAYBE I LEFT YOU HURTIN'
BUT BABY, I LOST MY PURPOSE.
CAN I GET A GODDAMN MINUTE?
THERE'S TOO MANY TIMES A DAY
WHERE I CAN'T EVEN THINK.

LILLI.

THERE'S A SOUND OF A CHAPTER ENDING	**THE GROUP.**
NOW.	AH
THERE'S A LINE IN BETWEEN THE STORIES.	
WE SHOULD READ OUT LOUD.	
IT SAYS TIME AND SPACE,	
THEY CAN'T REPLACE YOU.	AH
BUT YOU CAN'T	
ENGAGE.	EY

LILLI.
> I NEED YOU TO HELP ME TURN THE PAGE.
> WHAT IF THERE'S TIMES I STOP MYSELF FROM PUSHING SEND?
> MAKING THIS LOOK SO EASY WHEN IT'S ALL PRETEND.
> I KNOW IT MIGHT FEEL LONELY,
> BUT BABY, I'M JUST AS BROKEN.
> CAN WE GET A GODDAMN MINUTE?
> ISN'T IT CLEAR
> IT'S NOT JUST YOU WHO LOST A FRIEND?
> THERE'S A SOUND OF A CHAPTER ENDING NOW.
> THERE'S A LINE IN BETWEEN THE STORIES WE SHOULD READ OUT LOUD.
> IT SAYS TIME AND SPACE, THEY CAN'T REPLACE YOU.
> BUT YOU CAN'T ENGAGE.
> I NEED YOU TO HELP ME TURN THE PAGE.
> OO
> I'VE GOT A LITTLE MORE PAIN TO WORK THROUGH.
> WE CAN'T KEEP GUESSING WHAT IT'S ALL ABOUT.

THE GROUP.
> AH
>
>
> AH
>
> EY
> I NEED YOU TO HELP ME
> AH
> AH
> I'VE GOT A LITTLE MORE PAIN TO WORK THROUGH.

CLING TO THE SILENCE
WHERE WE LEARN TO
TRUST IT,
AND ON THE OTHER END
OF QUIET,
WE CAN LIVE OUT LOUD.
LIVE OUT LOUD.
THERE'S A SOUND OF A
CHAPTER ENDING NOW.
THERE'S A LINE IN
BETWEEN THE STORIES
WE SHOULD READ OUT
LOUD.

CLING TO THE SILENCE
WHERE WE LEARN TO
TRUST IT.

LOUD.

LILLI.
IT SAYS TIME AND
SPACE,
THEY CAN'T
REPLACE YOU.
BUT YOU CAN'T
ENGAGE.

GROUP 1.
TIME AND SPACE,

THEY CAN'T
REPLACE YOU.
BUT YOU CAN'T
ENGAGE.

GROUP 2.

AH

EY

LILLI.
I NEED YOU TO HELP ME
TURN THE PAGE.
I NEED YOU TO HELP ME
TURN THE PAGE.

THE GROUP.
I NEED YOU TO HELP ME
TURN THE PAGE.

(LILLI exits. NICK enters. They do not see or acknowledge each other.)

[MUSIC NO. 05 "I WISH I NEVER MET YOU"]

NICK.
I WISH I NEVER MET YOU
'CAUSE EVER SINCE THAT DAY
I FOUND MYSELF FALLING IN LOVE,
WHICH I WAS NEVER MEANT TO.
BUT THEN I WENT AND MET YOU.

NICK.
> NOW I'M STUCK UP IN THE CLOUDS
> UP ABOVE.
>
> I WISH I NEVER MET YOU,
> 'CAUSE I CAN BARELY WRITE A SONG
> WITHOUT STARTING TO WRITE DOWN YOUR NAME.
> SINCE OUR FIRST INTERACTION,
> YOU'VE BECOME MY WORST DISTRACTION.
> AND EVERY DAY SINCE HASN'T BEEN THE SAME.
>
> I WISH I NEVER GOT A GOOD LOOK AT YOU
> 'CAUSE EVERY TIME I CLOSE MY EYES,
> I SEE YOU LIKE YOU'RE THERE.
> THAT'S WHY I WISH I COULD SLEEP.
> MY EYES OPEN AT DAWN,
> EACH DAY REMINDS ME THAT YOU'RE GONE.
>
> I WISH I NEVER MET YOU
> SO THAT I COULD HAVE THE JOY
> OF MEETING YOU FOR THE FIRST TIME ONCE MORE.
> I WISH I NEVER MET YOU
> 'CAUSE NOW I CAN'T FORGET YOU.
> NOW EVERY NIGHT'S MORE SLEEPLESS THAN BEFORE.
> I WISH I NEVER MET YOU.
>
>> *(An immediate shift in energy...New York City. Rush hour. NICK gets swept up in a crowd racing for the subway.)*
>> **[MUSIC NO. 06 "THE THING I LIKE THE MOST ABOUT NEW YORK"]**
>
> THE THING I LIKE THE MOST ABOUT NEW YORK
> IS PROBABLY THE HOURS
> BETWEEN THREE O'CLOCK AND FIVE O'CLOCK.
> THE TRAIN TO TAKE YOU TWENTY BLOCKS
> IS VIOLENTLY CLOGGED UP WITH
> ALL THE HUNGRIEST AND CRANKIEST,

THE HAPPY ONES DON'T MAKE THE LIST.
FROM THREE TO FIVE, THE CITY'S PISSED.

> (**ALL** *brush past* **NICK** *to "exit" the "subway car."*)

AND THAT'S THE THING I LIKE THE MOST ABOUT NEW YORK.

LILLI.
THE THING I LIKE THE MOST ABOUT NEW YORK
IS WHEN DUMMIES FROM NEBRASKA
INTERRUPT ME JUST TO ASK
IF I COULD POINT THEM T'WARD SOME LANDMARK
THAT THEY'RE STANDING RIGHT THE FUCK IN FRONT OF.
I TURN AROUND, THERE'S NO EXCUSE.
I WALK AWAY, AND THEY'RE CONFUSED.
SO ALL IN ALL, I FEEL AMUSED.
AND THAT'S THE THING I LIKE THE MOST ABOUT NEW YORK.

RAY.
WAKING UP TO HONKING ON THE STREET.

THE GROUP.
BEEP BEEP!
BEEP BEEP! BEEP!

RAY.
WAY BEFORE YOU WANT!
THIS TOWN'S A BOMB WHO'S LOUDLY TICKING
THIS CITY ONLY KNOWS ONE WAY TO GREET YOU

	THE GROUP.
RAY. *(Spoken in rhythm.)*	OO OO
IT SAYS, "GOOD MORNING JERK!	WOP!
ARE THOSE YOUR NUTS?	
LOOKS LIKE THEY NEED A KICKING!"	
OW!	OW!

*(**THE GROUP** forms a "brunch tableau.")*

BONNIE.
>THE THING I LIKE THE MOST ABOUT NEW YORK
>IS THESE OVER-SEXED MILLENIALS
>TEXTING WHILE PRETENDING
>THEY ENJOY BRUNCHING FAR TOO MUCH
>WHILE SHOWING TONS OF SIDE BOOB.
>THE BROOKLYN CROWD DON'T GIVE A DAMN
>THEY DO IT ALL FOR INSTAGRAM.
>IT'S SOMETHING I DON'T UNDERSTAND

BONNIE.	**THE GROUP.**
AND THAT'S THE THING I LIKE	
THE MOST ABOUT NEW YORK.	MOS' 'BOUT

COLTON.
>BREAKING OUT WITH CANKER SORES FROM STRESS

THE GROUP.
>EW!
>GROSS!

COLTON.
>THE QUALITY OF LIFE IS JUST WHAT THE CITY'S SERVING.

COLTON.	**THE GROUP.**
THE PACE, THE LIFE, THE PEOPLE,	AH
AND THE MESS.	

COLTON.
>EVERY HEMORRHOID IS A BADGE OF HONOR
>THAT I'M SO DESERVING OF.

>*(**ALL** except **LILLI** freeze in a Times Square tableau.)*

LILLI.	**THE GROUP.**
SOMETIMES I GO TO TIMES SQUARE	AH
TO REMIND ME HOW LUCKY I AM.	
WHEN I DON'T FEEL LIKE I BELONG HERE,	

I LOOK STRAIGHT UP WHILE BASKING IN THE GLOW. THEN I GET THE FUCK RIGHT OUT OF THERE WHEN I SEE THAT RAPEY ELMO.	AH

THE GROUP.
THE THING I LIKE THE MOST ABOUT NEW YORK

>(**THE GROUP** *all begin cramming back into a "subway car."*)

COLTON.
IS THE FACT THAT WE ALL LOVE SO MUCH
THE THING THAT WE COMPLAIN ABOUT

BONNIE.
THERE NEVER REALLY WAS A DOUBT
WE'RE HERE 'CAUSE WE BELONG HERE.

NICK.	**THE GROUP.**
THIS CITY THRIVES ON ALL EXTREMES.	OO

RAY.
THIS CITY'S GREATER THAN IT SEEMS.   OO

LILLI.
THIS CITY'S FUCKIN' MADE OF DREAMS.   AH

THE GROUP.
AND THAT'S THE THING THAT I LIKE THE MOST ABOUT NEW YORK!

>(**THE GROUP** *sits in silence and looks at each other. Stillness. Silence.*)

>(**NICK** *subtly evaluates* **THE GROUP** *and thinks about speaking, but his mind is full of static. He remains seated.*)

[MUSIC NO. 07 "SOMETHING GOOD"]

>(**ALL** *exit except* **RAY.**)

RAY.
I THINK I'VE REACHED MY CAP.

RAY.
>I THINK I'VE MET MY LIMIT.
>NO MORE SMILING THROUGH THE CRAP YOU PUT ME THROUGH.
>I ALWAYS DO.
>DON'T ACT LIKE YOU'RE ALL THAT.
>I'VE SEEN SOME NASTY WEATHER
>WHEN YOU USED TO HAVE MY BACK
>AND SHIT WAS TIGHT TOGETHER.
>
>WHEN WE KNEW IT WAS SOMETHING GOOD.
>YOU HAD SOMEONE WHO UNDERSTOOD.
>
>NOW I CAN'T GO ON PRETENDING
>THAT YOU'RE ACTING LIKE YOU SHOULD,
>BUT I'M HERE BECAUSE I KNOW
>YOU'LL GROW BACK INTO SOMETHING GOOD.
>
>YOUR FABRICATIONS STACK.
>THEY GROW INTO A PILE
>WHILE YOU WEAR THAT SILLY MASK
>AND PLAY PRETEND.
>
>YOUR FORTRESS STARTS TO CRACK
>I SEE YOU AND I KNOW
>I LIKED YOU BEST WHEN YOU WERE FAT.
>YOU USED TO KNOW EXACTLY WHO YOU WERE.
>
>IT WAS SOMETHING GOOD.
>YOU HAD FRIENDS WHO ALL UNDERSTOOD.
>
>BUT NOW I CAN'T GO ON PRETENDING
>THAT YOU'RE ACTING LIKE YOU SHOULD.
>I'M STILL HERE BECAUSE I HOPE
>YOU'LL GROW BACK INTO SOMETHING GOOD.
>
>SIT THROUGH SHALLOW CONVERSATION.
>TALK TO THE WALL...
>I MIGHT AS WELL THOUGH.
>WHO KNEW YOU COULD TAKE THE ONLY MOMENT THAT I NEEDED
>AND MAKE IT SOMETHING THAT WAS ALL ABOUT YOU?

BECAUSE THE TRUTH IS THAT I'M WATCHING
FROM A PLACE WHERE YOU ONCE STOOD
AND I'M LOSING SIGHT OF WHO YOU WERE,
THE SIGHT OF SOMETHING GOOD.

> *(**RAY** takes a beat and exits. **COLTON** enters. They do not see or acknowledge each other.)*
>
> **[MUSIC NO. 08 "LITTLE SISTER"]**
>
> *(**COLTON** is in a "hospital room" looking at his new little sister for the first time.)*

COLTON.
LITTLE SISTER.
SLEEPING SOUNDLY.
TRYING NOT TO WAKE HER.
TINY MOVEMENTS.
SO ASTOUNDING.
PROMISE I WON'T BREAK HER.

I'M WAITING FOR MY TURN
TO HOLD HER LIKE YOU TAUGHT ME.
ONE ARM TO CRADLE,
THE OTHER HOLDS HER HEAD.
I CAN SEE HER START TO OPEN HER EYES.
DOES SHE KNOW I'M HER BROTHER YET?
MM

LITTLE SISTER
NEEDS ATTENTION.
SHOULDN'T BE A PROBLEM.
WE LOOK SO MUCH
LIKE EACH OTHER,
BUT DON'T HAVE MUCH IN COMMON.

I'M WAITING FOR MY TURN
TO TEACH YOU SOMETHING USEFUL,
THE SAME WAY THAT DANNY TAUGHT ME HOW TO PLAY.
THEN MAYBE YOU'LL REMEMBER
FOR WHEN YOU'RE AN OLDER SISTER –

COLTON.
>YOU'LL HAVE SOMETHING
>TO TEACH THEM ONE DAY.

	THE GROUP.
COLTON.	AH
OH	
	AH
OH	
	AH
WHOA	
	AH

COLTON.
>LITTLE SISTER
>JUST FOUND OUT
>SHE'LL HAVE A LITTLE SISTER.
>LITTLE SISTER,
>SLIGHTLY JEALOUS,
>PLANNING TO DISMISS HER.
>I PROMISE YOU WILL SEE
>THE GIFT THAT YOU ARE GETTING –
>ANOTHER FRIEND TO LEAN ON,
>OR EVEN JUST TO BLAME.
>SO TRY TO GET TO KNOW HER
>DANNY AND I CAN TELL YOU
>YOUR LIFE WILL NEVER BE THE SAME.
>
>TIME TO SEE YOUR LITTLE SISTER.
>SHE CAN'T WAIT TO MEET YOU.
>JUST LIKE YOU,
>SHE CAME OUT SINGING.
>PERFECT WAY TO GREET YOU.
>NOW YOU'RE WAITING FOR YOUR TURN
>TO HOLD HER LIKE MOM SHOWED US.
>ONE ARM TO CRADLE
>THE OTHER HOLDS HER HEAD.
>YOU CAN SEE HER START TO OPEN HER EYES.

DOES SHE KNOW WE'RE HER FAMILY YET?
OH...
OH OH

> (**COLTON** *exits. Lights up on* **BONNIE** *in a beautiful tableau supported by the cast.*)
>
> (**BONNIE** *is on a proverbial pedestal.*)
>
> **[MUSIC NO. 09 "FAKING COOL"]**

BONNIE & THE GROUP.
I WAS NEVER THE COOL KID GROWING UP.
I WAS LIKED JUST WELL ENOUGH.
CREATING SPACE TO FIND ESCAPE IN MAKING TOO MUCH SOUND.
NO HICKIES ON MY NECK,
NEVER TRIED OUT CIGARETTES.
I MADE SOME FRIENDS,
I MADE SOME MUSIC,
THEN I WROTE IT DOWN.

> (**THE GROUP** *fades away, leaving* **BONNIE** *alone and vulnerable.*)

BONNIE.
NEVER TOLD ENOUGH OF A STORY.
NEVER FELT THE RIGHT TO COMPLAIN.
I ALWAYS FELT LIKE A CUL-DE-SAC,
AND MY KIND OF UPBRINGING COULD'VE HELD ME BACK.
ARTISTS FROM THE SUBURBS ARE SO DUMB TO EXPLAIN
'CAUSE THERE'S MUCH MORE TO LIFE
THAN WHAT'S BLACK AND WHITE.
CAN'T STAY WAITING FOR THE COLORS TO APPEAR.

THE GROUP.
WHOA WHOA OO

BONNIE.
HAVE ME FIGURED OUT,
NOT A BIT OF DOUBT.

THE GROUP.
>WHOA WHOA OO

BONNIE.
>WELL GUESS AGAIN, BECAUSE YOU HAVE THE WRONG IDEA.

>>*(The voices that once supported her turn on her. There's a sense of conflict, mockery, and intimidation from **THE GROUP**.)*

BONNIE.	**THE GROUP.**
I'M FAKING IT FOR YOU.	OO OH
I'M FAKING IT FOR YOU.	OO OH
EVERYTHING I DO COMES FROM A BORROWED SET OF TOOLS.	I'M FAKING COOL,
I'M FAKING IT FOR YOU.	I'M FAKING COOL,
HOW COULD I BE YOUR IDEA OF COOL?	I'M FAKING COOL.

BONNIE.
>I ALWAYS THINK IT'S CLOSE TO OUTRAGEOUS
>YOU CAN'T TELL I'M INSECURE.
>I GUESS MY GRIN IS A GIVEAWAY
>THAT I'M FEELING LIKE A WINNER WHO CAN LIVE TODAY,
>BUT SEE UP CLOSE THAT I'M SO PAINFULLY UNSURE.

BONNIE.	**THE GROUP.**
GUESS YOUR MIND IS MADE,	HAH WAH
CALL A SPADE A SPADE,	HAH WAH
CAN'T STAY WAITING FOR THE TRUTH TO COME TO YOU.	HAH WAH
	HAH WAH
	WHOA WHOA OO
HAVE ME FIGURED OUT, CAN'T HEAR ME WHEN I SHOUT,	WHOA WHOA OO

THE TRUTH IS THAT YOU	
HAVEN'T GOT A CLUE	WAH
I'M FAKING IT FOR YOU.	OO OH
I'M FAKING IT FOR YOU.	OO OH
EVERYTHING I DO	
COMES FROM A BORROWED	I'M FAKIN' COOL,
SET OF TOOLS.	I'M FAKIN' COOL,
I'M FAKING IT FOR YOU.	I'M FAKIN' COOL.
HOW COULD I BE YOUR IDEA OF COOL?	

BONNIE.
IT TAKES A LOT TO WRITE A STORY,
A NEED THAT'S SOMETIMES OUT OF PLACE.
I'LL WRITE IT OUT ABOUT THE STRUGGLES AND THE GLORY,
AND WEAR A SMILE ON MY FACE.

BONNIE.	**THE GROUP.**
BUT I DON'T UNDERSTAND	AH
A WORD I'M SAYING.	
NO, I'M SHOOTING IN THE DARK AND I	
START PRAYING	OH

BONNIE.
THAT YOU CONTINUE THINKING
THAT I'M THE GUY YOU ALWAYS THOUGHT I WAS.

(The voices shift from intimidation to solidarity.)

'CAUSE THERE'S MUCH MORE TO LIFE
THAN WHAT'S BLACK AND WHITE.

BONNIE.	
CAN'T STAY WAITING FOR THE COLORS TO APPEAR.	**THE GROUP.**
	WHOA WHOA OO

BONNIE.
> HAVE ME FIGURED OUT,
> NOT A BIT OF DOUBT.
> WELL, GUESS AGAIN,
>   BECAUSE YOU

THE GROUP.

BONNIE.	THE GROUP.
HAVE THE WROING IDEA.	AH
I'M FAKING IT FOR YOU	OH
I'M FAKING IT FOR YOU	OH OH
EVERYTHING I DO	OH
COMES FROM A BORROWED	
SET OF TOOLS.	
I'M FAKING IT FOR YOU	OH OH
I'M FAKING IT FOR YOU	
	I'M FAKING COOL,
I'M FAKING IT FOR YOU	I'M FAKIN' IT NOW.
	I'M FAKING COOL,
EVERYTHING I DO	I'M FAKIN' IT NOW.
COMES FROM A BORROWED SET OF TOOLS	I'M FAKING COOL,
I'M FAKING IT FOR YOU	I'M FAKIN' IT NOW.
	I'M FAKING COOL.
HOW COULD I BE YOUR IDEA OF COOL?	

(LILLI, COLTON, NICK, and BONNIE all exit, leaving RAY alone in his chair.)

[MUSIC NO. 10 "I'M NOT FALLING FOR THAT"]

RAY.
> SHE SAYS THAT I'M DRAMATIC
> AS IF I DIDN'T KNOW.
> BUT MAYBE THROUGH THESE DAMN DRAMATIC TANTRUMS
> I HAVE NOWHERE LEFT TO GO,

HEY, IT'S PROBLEMATIC.
THE BATTLE COMES FROM LOVE.
THE MASK AND MULTITASKING EVERY PASSION,
ALL PUSH THAT TURNS TO SHOVE.

LET'S BREAK THE MOLD
WE'RE GOING NOWHERE

WE TOOK THE LONG LONG LONG WAY AROUND
IT WAS THE WRONG WRONG WRONG WAY
TO TELL YOU I WAS DROWNING
GET UP OFF OF THAT CELL PHONE,
GIVE ME MORE THAN A "HELL NO"
REBUILD THIS CONVERSATION

RAY.	**THE GROUP.**
I'M NOT FALLING FOR THAT.	AH
THE FIGHT BECOMES ROBOTIC.	
IT'S ONE WE'VE HAD BEFORE	
I TAKE A LEAP JUST	
HOPING EVERY MISFIRE	OO
GETS SWEPT UP OR IGNORED	
HEY IT'S IDIOTIC	AH
THE WAY WE CIRCLE BACK,	AH
SCREAMING LIKE WE MEAN IT,	
CAN'T BELIEVE IT	
THERE'S NO CAUSE	
FOR THE ATTACK,	AH
WHOA NO.	
LET'S BREAK THE MOLD	OH
WE'RE GOING NOWHERE	NO
WE TOOK THE LONG LONG LONG WAY AROUND	
IT WAS THE WRONG WRONG WRONG WAY	
TO TELL YOU I WAS DROWNING	AH

RAY.

GET UP OFF OF THAT CELL PHONE.
GIVE ME MORE THAN A "HELL NO"

RAY.
> REBUILD THIS CONVERSATION
> I'M NOT FALLING.
>
> I'LL WAIT FOR THE SIGNAL
> FORGET AND FORGIVE.
> THERE'S A BETTER WAY TO LIVE.
> IT'S AS SMALL AS A THIMBLE,
> THEN WHY'S IT SO BIG?

RAY.	**THE GROUP.**
GIVE ME MORE SLAMMING DOORS!	AH
YEAH!	
SOMETIMES IT'S HARD TO BELIEVE THAT	
WE'LL EVER DEFEAT THAT	AW
VILLAIN OUT FOR BLOOD	
	AH

RAY.
> BUT WE GOT THIS.
> YEAH, WE GOT THIS.
>
> NOT TO GET POETIC,
> BUT YOU MAY NEVER KNOW
> HOW EVERY TIME I SEE YOU

RAY.	**THE GROUP.**
EVEN DAYLIGHT CAN'T OUTSHINE	AH
YOUR GLOW.	

RAY.
> WE TOOK THE LONG LONG LONG WAY AROUND
> IT WAS THE WRONG WRONG WRONG WAY

RAY.	**THE GROUP.**
TO TELL YOU I WAS DROWNING.	AH
GET UP OFF THE CELL PHONE,	
GIVE ME MORE THAN A "HELL NO."	
REBUILD THIS CONVERSATION.	
I'M NOT FALLING	
FOR THAT.	AH

> (**THE GROUP** *slowly sits in silence and looks at each other. This silence is a bit more relaxed, but still very awkward...*)
>
> (**NICK** *evaluates the other four in* **THE GROUP**. **NICK**, *seated, takes a breath.*)

NICK. I wrote a note...

> (**THE GROUP** *turns to give focus to* **NICK**. **NICK** *feels this shift. He tries to keep talking, but he can't. His mind is full of static.*)
>
> (*A beat...*)
>
> **[MUSIC NO. 11 "ON AND ON AND ON..."]**

BONNIE.
IT'S DEPRESSING TO THINK
HOW COURAGEOUS I WAS
NOT TOO LONG AGO.
IT'S IMPRESSIVE TO THINK
I WAS NEVER AFRAID
TO GO OUT ON A LIMB.
BUT WHAT DID I KNOW?

I HAD HIGH HOPES
AND I HAD LOW PRESSURE.
I HAD NO FEAR.
LIFE WAS DESIGNED MESSILY,
STRESSES WOULD ROLL OFF MY BACK,
AND SO
ON AND ON AND ON AND ON I'D GO.

> (**LILLI** *quietly enters. She and* **BONNIE** *share the stage but can't see each other.*)

LILLI.
IT'S AMAZING TO ME
HOW I GOT THIS FAR
WITHOUT KNOWING A THING.
IT'S AMAZING TO SEE

LILLI.
> THE THINGS THAT I HAVE
> WERE ONCE IN A PLACE
> THAT SEEMED SO OUT OF REACH.
>
> I HAD HIGH GOALS
> AND I HAD LOW INCOME.
> I HAD NO DOUBTS.
> LIFE WAS DESIGNED SLOPPILY,
> STOPPING WAS NEVER A THOUGHT,
> AND SO
> ON AND ON AND ON AND ON I'D GO.

BONNIE & LILLI.
> I USED TO HAVE EYES
> THAT WOULD LIGHT UP WITH WONDER.
> I'D SHOUT TO THE SKIES,
> I HAD A ROAR LOUDER THAN THUNDER.

BONNIE.
> AND NOW IT'S JUST NOISE.

LILLI.
> AND PRAYING FOR BUZZ.
>
> *(**BONNIE** and **LILLI** make eye contact. They connect for a few breaths.)*

BONNIE & LILLI.
> AND MISSING THE PERSON I WAS.

BONNIE.
> IT'S DISTRESSING TO THINK
> I'VE LOST WHAT IT TAKES
> TO BECOME SOMETHING NEW.

LILLI.
> IT'S A BLESSING TO THINK
> THAT I'VE STILL MORE TO GIVE.

BONNIE & LILLI.
BELIEVE IT OR NOT,
THERE'S STILL MORE TO DO.

I HAVE HIGH HOPES
AND NO WORRIES
BECAUSE I KNOW
LIFE FLIES BY IN A HURRY
IF WE DON'T SLOW DOWN TO LIVE.

BONNIE.
STILL ON AND ON...

LILLI.
AND ON AND ON...

BONNIE & LILLI.
WE GO.
LA DA DA
DA DA DA
DA DA DA
DA DA DA.

> (**BONNIE** and **LILLI** exit.)
>
> (**COLTON** enters. An empty chair from the **THE GROUP** circle makes him think about his father's favorite chair from home.)

[MUSIC NO. 12 "THE ESSENCE OF GEORGE"]

COLTON.
GEORGE AND KELLY MARRIED,
BARELY OLD ENOUGH TO DRINK.
EVERY DAY SINCE THEY'D BEEN DATING
A LIFE TOGETHER IS ALL HE'D THINK OF.
STARTED HAVING BABIES,
FOUR NEW MOUTHS THEY HAVE TO FEED.
NEVER-ENDING NOISE.
TWO LOUD GIRLS, TWO LOUD BOYS.

COLTON.
>NAVIGATING LIFE WITHOUT A CLUE.
>THE BABIES RAISING BABIES
>ALWAYS GUESSING WHAT TO DO.
>
>HERE WE ARE,
>GETTING BY ON ONLY STREET SMARTS.
>HERE WE ARE,
>JUST A PAIR OF HIGH SCHOOL SWEETHEARTS.
>I DON'T KNOW HOW THE HELL WE MAKE IT WORK,
>THIS FAMILY WE ARE BUILDING FROM THE GROUND.
>
>GEORGE IS ALWAYS WORKING
>BUT HE CHECKS IN WHEN HE CAN.
>EVERY DAY IS JUST ANOTHER DAY
>OF GETTING HIS ASS HANDED TO HIM.

COLTON.	**THE GROUP.**
COUNTING DOWN THE HOURS	AH

COLTON.
>TILL HE'S BACK HOME WITH HIS FAMILY
>YEAH, THE JOB MIGHT KILL
>BUT HE KNOWS THE DRILL.
>
>PUSHING THROUGH THIS HELL JUST TO PROVIDE.
>WORK TO FIND THE TIME FOR PRIDEFUL CHEERING
>FROM THE SIDELINES.

THE GROUP.
>HERE WE ARE,

COLTON.
>WITH OUR HEAD ABOVE WATER.

THE GROUP.
>HERE WE ARE,

COLTON.
>WITH TWO SONS AND TWO DAUGHTERS.

THE GROUP.
>NO ONE'S SURE

COLTON.
> HOW THE HELL WE MAKE IT WORK,
> THIS FAMILY WE'VE BUILT UP FROM THE GROUND,
> THIS FAMILY WE BUILT UP FROM THE GROUND.

COLTON.	**THE GROUP.**
GEORGE COULD BE A RAMBUNCTIOUS ONE ON THE GO.	AH

COLTON.
> THE STRESS AND EXCESS OF A MAN WITH A FAMILY
> FINDING NEW REASONS TO SLOW DOWN
> A WHITE-COLLAR MAN WITH A BLUE-COLLAR HEART

COLTON.	**THE GROUP.**
AND A LOVE THAT HAS NOT MET ITS BOUNDS	AH

COLTON.
> EVEN WHEN HE GETS KICKED TO THE GROUND
> HE COMES TO HIS FAMILY WHERE HE KNOWS A SMILE CAN BE FOUND.
>
> DAD TAUGHT ME YOUNG
> TO WORK HARD FOR THE THINGS THAT I WANTED.
> SO I STRAPPED A GUITAR TO MY BACK AND LEFT HOME
> TO GET THIS SILLY CAREER STARTED.
> LIFTED ME UP TO MAKE SURE I WAS OUT THERE,
> GATHERING STORIES TO TELL.
> HE WOULD SHARE HIS OWN STORIES AS WELL.
> HE JUST WANTED TO MAKE SURE I WOKE UP EACH DAY
> DOING THE THING THAT I LOVED.
> AND TO

THE GROUP.
> GROW

COLTON.
> OH…

COLTON.
>GEORGE AND KELLY VISIT
>PROBABLY MUCH MORE THAN MOST.
>HIS KIDS ALL MAKE HIM PROUD.
>IT'S HIS BICOASTAL WAY OF BOASTING.
>GEORGE'S VERY FIRST BORN
>HAS A FIRST BORN OF HIS OWN.
>AS HIS FAMILY GROWS
>HE FINALLY KNOWS...
>
>HERE WE ARE
>AFTER RAISING ALL THESE DREAMERS.
>THERE THEY GO
>WITH THE PURPOSE THEY ALL FOUND.
>AND ALL I KNOW IS GEORGE GOT EVERYTHING HE WANTED:
>THIS FAMILY HE BUILT UP FROM THE GROUND,

COLTON.	**THE GROUP.**
THIS FAMILY HE BUILT UP FROM THE GROUND.	AH
MM	

>(**COLTON** *false-exits to join* **NICK** *and* **THE GROUP,** *who have subtly entered.*)
>
>**[MUSIC NO. 13 "WHAT THE HELL AM I DOING WITH MY LIFE?"]**

NICK.	**THE GROUP.**
AND CAN YOU BELIEVE IT?	OO
I'M STILL A MOTHER FUCKING OPTIMIST	
AFTER ALL THE TIMES I'VE SEEN IT TURN TO SHIT.	OO
BUT	

NICK & THE GROUP.
>I'M STILL SMILING
>SO PEOPLE LIKE TO CALL ME OPTIMISTIC.

NICK.
WELL IF

NICK & THE GROUP.
I'M SO GODDAMN OPTIMISTIC,

NICK.
THEN

NICK & THE GROUP.
WHY DO I WANT TO CALL IT QUITS?

> *(Energy shifts to something slightly more chaotic.)*

RAY.
HOW GREAT THAT I GOT TO MEET YOU,
LET ME CHANGE YOUR LIFE.
I HAVE ALL THE ANSWERS THAT YOU'RE LOOKING FOR.
DON'T GO ON THINKING THAT THIS KITCHEN'S GONNA CLOSE.
I'M THE CHEF AND YOU'RE JUST WHO I'M COOKING FOR.
I'M FEEDING EVERYONE EXACTLY WHAT I'M CRAVING
I NEVER TASTE THE FOOD, SO TELL ME WHOSE LIFE AM I SAVING?
OH WHAT THE HELL

THE GROUP.
OH WHAT THE HELL

RAY & THE GROUP.
AM I DOING WITH MY LIFE?

RAY.
OH WHAT THE HELL

THE GROUP.
OH WHAT THE HELL

RAY & THE GROUP.
AM I DOING WITH MY LIFE?

RAY.
> FAKING IT WELL,

THE GROUP.
> FAKING IT WELL,

RAY.
> I'LL NEVER TELL

THE GROUP.
> I'LL NEVER TELL

RAY.
> THAT IT'S RUINING MY LIFE.

LILLI.
> I SENSE YOU'RE TROUBLED,
> COME ON, LET ME LEND AN EAR.
> ANYTHING TO QUIET DOWN
> THE MONSTERS IN MY HEAD.
> YOU MADE SOME BAD DECISIONS,
> THAT'S WHAT YOU'VE MADE CLEAR.
> THE DEVIL'S ON YOUR SHOULDER,
> BUT THE ANGEL STAYED IN BED.

LILLI.
> I'M

LILLI, NICK & COLTON.
> GIVING EVERYONE EXACTLY WHAT THEY'RE NEEDING.

LILLI.
> I'LL STITCH UP EVERY WOUND YOU HAVE
> WHILE I'M JUST LEFT HERE BLEEDING.
> OH WHAT THE HELL

THE GROUP.
> OH WHAT THE HELL

LILLI & THE GROUP.
> AM I DOING WITH MY LIFE?

LILLI.
>OH WHAT THE HELL

THE GROUP.
>OH WHAT THE HELL

LILLI & THE GROUP.
>AM I DOING WITH MY LIFE?

LILLI.
>I'M FAKING IT WELL,

THE GROUP.
>FAKING IT WELL,

LILLI.
>I'LL NEVER TELL

THE GROUP.
>I'LL NEVER TELL

LILLI.
>THAT I'M RUINING MY LIFE

COLTON.	**THE GROUP.**
CHASING AFTER DREAMS SINCE I WAS FIVE. DREAMS DON'T ALL MAKE MONEY, BUT THEY'RE KEEPING ME ALIVE.	DAT DAT DAT DAT AHHH DAT DAT DAT DAT

RAY.

FOCUSING ON EVERYBODY ELSE, I'LL JUST KEEP ON HELPING EVERYBODY BUT MYSELF.	DAT DAT DAT DAT AHHH

NICK.
>WHAT THE HELL AM I...

COLTON.
>WHAT THE HELL AM I...

LILLI.
WHAT THE HELL AM I...

RAY & THE GROUP.
WHAT THE HELL AM I DOING?

BONNIE.
OH WHAT THE HELL

THE GROUP.
OH WHAT THE HELL

BONNIE & THE GROUP.
AM I DOING WITH MY LIFE?

BONNIE.
NO

> *(We take the lid off the rage and anxiety that we spend every day suppressing for one sweet, sloppy "dance break.")*

OH WHAT THE HELL

THE GROUP.
OH WHAT THE HELL

BONNIE & THE GROUP.
AM I DOING WITH MY LIFE?

BONNIE.
WHAT AM I DOING WITH MY LIFE?
FAKING IT WELL,

THE GROUP.
FAKING IT WELL,

BONNIE.
I'LL NEVER TELL

THE GROUP.
I'LL NEVER TELL.

BONNIE.
THAT I'M RUINING MY LIFE.

THE GROUP.
>WHOA OO WHOA
>WHOA OO WHOA
>AH AH

>*(**THE GROUP** sits in a more relaxed, comfortable silence than what we've seen.)*
>*(**NICK** evaluates **THE GROUP**, hoping to speak.)*
>*(He stands, takes a breath.)*

NICK. I wrote a note for my parents to see. Saying that…

>*(The static in **NICK**'s head gets too loud.)*

I'm sorry I can't.

>*(**NICK** sits in his chair. A beat…)*
>*(**ALL** remain seated onstage. Focus to **BONNIE**.)*

[MUSIC NO. 14 "CAUGHT IN A LOOP"]

BONNIE.
>SO MUCH TIME LEFT WAITING,
>SO MANY DAYS JUST HANGING ON TO WHAT FELL APART,
>CONTEMPLATING
>SHOULD I WASTE AWAY
>WAITING FOR MY OWN PURPOSE TO START?

>THE WEED HELPS ME NEGLECT THE SEARCH FOR
>WHO I NEED TO BE.
>AND DRINKING HELPS FORGET THE EFFORT
>NEEDED TO BE ME.

>WISHING ON A FOUR-LEAF CLOVER
>WHEN I SHOULD BE STARTING OVER.
>IT'S LIKE I'M CAUGHT UP IN A LOOP,
>CAUGHT UP IN A LOOP,
>I CAN'T SEEM TO BREAK THIS HABIT.
>WISHING ON A FOUR-LEAF CLOVER.

>I THINK THE PAINT'S DONE DRYING.
>I'VE BEEN WATCHING THESE WALLS

BONNIE.
    AS IF THEY'LL SAY SOMETHING NEW.
    BARELY TRYING.
    AM I WAITING FOR A CALLING
    WHILE I STALL TO GIVE ME SOMETHING TO DO?
    PROCRASTINATING HELPS REMIND ME
    I SHOULD JUST GET STONED.
    AND MASTURBATING HELPS REMIND ME
    THAT I'M HERE ALONE.
    WISHING ON A FOUR-LEAF CLOVER,

BONNIE.	**THE GROUP (MEN).**
WHEN I SHOULD BE STARTING OVER.	OO AH
IT'S LIKE I'M	**THE GROUP.**
CAUGHT UP IN A LOOP,	I'M CAUGHT IN A LOOP,
C-CAUGHT IN A LOOP,	C-CAUGHT IN A LOOP,
I CAN'T SEEM TO BREAK THIS HABIT.	AH
WISHING ON A FOUR-LEAF CLOVER.	AH

BONNIE.
    I'VE BEEN DEPENDENT ON LUCK
    FOR A LITTLE WHILE NOW

BONNIE.	**THE GROUP.**
	AH
I'VE BEEN TOO COMFORTABLE WITH THINGS	OO
FOR A LITTLE WHILE NOW	OO
I SHOUDN'T HAVE TO BE SCARED	AH
THAT I'VE LOST THE GOODS	OO
OH I KNOW THAT THERE'S A GAME TO PLAY.	AH
BUT FOR TODAY,	

BONNIE.
    I'M WISHING ON A FOUR-LEAF CLOVER,
    WHEN I SHOULD BE STARTING OVER.

BONNIE.	THE GROUP.
ITS LIKE I'M CAUGHT UP IN A LOOP,	I'M CAUGHT UP IN A LOOP,
CAUGHT UP IN A LOOP,	CAUGHT UP IN A LOOP,

BONNIE.
I CAN'T SEEM TO BREAK THIS HABIT.
WISHING ON A FOUR-LEAF CLOVER

(THE GROUP remains seated in their respective chairs and listens to COLTON.)
[MUSIC NO. 15 "MOM COULD PLAY GUITAR"]

COLTON.
MOM CAME HOME WITH LOTS TO SAY.
SHE'S PISSED BECAUSE SHE FOUND A GRAY HAIR.
YOU'D NEVER GUESS THAT SHE'D AGED A DAY...
BUT SOMETIMES LIFE JUST DOESN'T PLAY FAIR.

MY MOM AND DAD LOVED PDA.
HE SHARED THE JOY TRUE LOVE COULD BRING HER.
THEY MADE A HOME NORTH OF THE BAY.
MY MOM SHOWED ME HOW TO BE A SINGER.
MUSIC WAS LIKE BREATHING, 'CAUSE IT LOOKED SO EASY.
SHE ALWAYS HAD A SONG WORTH SINGING.

MOM TAUGHT MUSIC EVERY DAY
AND RAISED US ALL BY THE WESTERN SEABOARD.
WHEN I TOLD MOM THAT I WANT TO PLAY
SHE GRABBED HER GUITAR,
TAUGHT ME A D CHORD.

HER CALLOUSED FINGERS
MADE IT LOOK SO EASY.
THANKS FOR BEING PATIENT WITH ME.

OOH, THE ONLY MUSIC I KNEW
WAS FROM DAYS OF EACH AMAZING CHILDHOOD AFTERNOON.
AND, OOH, JUST TAKE A LOOK AT WHERE WE ARE.
IT'S ALL BECAUSE MY MOM COULD PLAY GUITAR.

COLTON.
>AFTER SCHOOL SHE WAS THE CARPOOL QUEEN.
>FOUR LOUD KIDS... SHE'D NEVER BE BORED.
>I WAS A SHITHEAD ANGSTY TEEN,
>FIXATED ON A LIFE LED BY A D CHORD.
>
>PUTTING WORDS TO MUSIC,
>IT WASN'T ALWAYS EASY,
>BUT MOM WAS ALWAYS THERE BELIEVING.
>
>OOH, THE ONLY MUSIC I KNEW
>WAS FROM DAYS OF EACH AMAZING CHILDHOOD AFTERNOON.
>AND, OOH, THE MUSIC LED ME SO FAR...
>AND IT'S ALL BECAUSE MY MOM COULD PLAY GUITAR.

COLTON.	**THE GROUP.**
ONE THING I LEARNED,	AH
JUST BY BEING AROUND:	
A MOTHER'S JOB IS NEVER FINISHED,	AH
EVEN WHEN WE'RE GROWN.	

COLTON.
>AND THERE'S NOTHING LIKE THE WOUND SHE GETS
>FROM HEARING THE WORDS:
>"I NEED TO DO THIS ON MY OWN."
>
>MOM'S WORST FEAR: THE EMPTY NEST...
>A HOUSE FULL GONE MUST HIT THE HARDEST.
>MOM AND DAD CAN ONLY DO THEIR BEST.

COLTON.	**THE GROUP.**
THE PLIGHT OF RAISING FOUR YOUNG ARTISTS.	MM

COLTON.
>MOM TAUGHT ME TO BE BRAVE,
>'CAUSE WHAT YOU FEAR IS WHAT YOU LEAN TOWARD.
>YEARS OF SACRIFICE AND SAVINGS
>I NEVER THANKED HER FOR THE D CHORD.

(THE GROUP *remains seated. Light pans across their faces, landing on* **RAY.**)
[MUSIC NO. 16 "SNOW"]

RAY.
I FOUND ROCK-BOTTOM
AT SIX O'CLOCK TODAY.
WOKE UP TO SNOWFLAKES
LANDING ON MY FACE.
LAST NIGHT'S FORGOTTEN,
EACH MEMORY'S ERASED.
I FOUND ROCK-BOTTOM
AT PARK AND 88TH.
AND YOU KNOW HOW I GET LOW
ON MY NIGHTS WITHOUT YOU.
SO I'LL GO
WHEREVER YOU ARE.
THE GUILT COMES CALLING
AM I BEING SOMEONE ELSE?
AM I LETTING DOWN THE YOUNGER VERSIONS OF MYSELF?
FORGET THAT FEELING
I'LL JUST FUEL MY BRAIN WITH LIGHTENING.
I'M SCARED OF HEIGHTS,
BUT COMING DOWN SEEMS MUCH MORE FRIGHTENING.
AND I KNOW I'LL BE FINE WITHOUT YOU.
PLEASE DON'T GO

THE GROUP.
OH

RAY.
DON'T GO
LEAVING ME HERE IN THE SNOW.
THIS IS NOT NECESSARILY SOME FUN KIND OF SONG
THAT I WANT MY MOM HEARING ABOUT ME.

RAY.
    'CAUSE SHE DID NOTHING WRONG.
    IT'S IMPORTANT SHE KNOWS
    IT WAS MY FAULT.
    I WANTED TO TRY COCAINE,

THE GROUP.
OH OO
OH OO AH
OH OO AH
OH OO AH
OH OO AH

RAY.
    'CAUSE IT FOOLS YOU WITH HOPE,
    A FALSE SENSE OF BELIEF IN YOURSELF
    WHEN YOU RUN OUT OF FAITH.
    UNTIL YOU WAKE UP IN A SNOWBANK
    AT PARK AND 88TH.

THE GROUP.
    OH OO AH
    OO OO OO
    MM MM

RAY.
    THIS IS NOT NECESSARILY
    SOME FUN KIND OF SONG
    THAT I WANT MY MOM HEARING ABOUT ME.

    (The song ends with everyone's focus on **RAY**.*)*
    (**LILLI** *holds her focus on* **RAY**...*)*
    [MUSIC NO. 17 "WE AREN'T KIDS ANYMORE"]

LILLI.
    EVER TRY TO REMEMBER BEING A KID?
    THERE'S A LOT THAT I LIKED ABOUT BEING A KID.
    OPINIONS ARE FACTS,
    NO STRESS ABOUT TAXES OR DEATH.

    I COULD PLAY EVERY DAY WITHOUT BREAKING A SWEAT,
    LIKE A WAY OF ESCAPING WHAT I DIDN'T GET.
    ESCAPING MEANT HIDING FROM LIFE
    AND PLAYING PRETEND.

AVOIDING THE PART WHERE IT ALL HAS TO END.
DON'T MATTER HOW FAST OR SLOW,
EVERYBODY HAS TO GROW UP.

AND JUST LIKE THAT, YOU FEEL LOST,
TRYING TO FIGURE OUT JUST WHERE TO GO.
WHAT CAN YOU DO WHEN YOU'RE TOSSED
IN THE MIDDLE OF THIS SO-CALLED NORMAL
WITH THE LITTLE YOU KNOW.

LILLI.	**THE GROUP.**
NO MORE TIME FOR GAMES	AH
AND EVERY DAY'S THE SAME JUST AS BEFORE.	HAH
CLOSER TO UNDERSTANDING	AH HAH

LILLI.

WE AREN'T KIDS ANYMORE.

EVERY NOW AND AGAIN
I'M REMINDED OF SOMETHING THAT'S GONE.
GAMES AREN'T AS FUN
WHEN YOU'RE SOMEONE SOMEBODY COUNTS ON.
OPINIONS DON'T MATTER.
WELL, EITHER THAT OR MUCH WORSE.

BUT WHO CARES,
NO ONE'S THERE TO SAY "YOU'RE DOING FINE."
SIT AND STARE
UNTIL THERE'S SOMEONE'S HELP TO DECLINE.
ESCAPING MEANS RUNNING AWAY

THE GROUP.

HAH

LILLI.

AND MISSING MY YOUTH.
WE LIVE DAY BY DAY,

LILLI.	**THE GROUP.**
ACCEPTING THE TRUTH –	AH

LILLI.
> NO MATTER HOW FAST OR SLOW,
> EVERYBODY HAS TO GROW UP.
>
> AND JUST LIKE THAT YOU FEEL LOST,
> TRYING TO FIGURE OUT WHAT WENT SO WRONG.
> WHAT CAN YOU DO WHEN YOU'RE TOSSED
> IN THE MIDDLE OF THIS SO-CALLED NORMAL
> WHERE YOU NEVER BELONGED.

LILLI.	**THE GROUP.**
JUST KEEP HOLDING ON,	AH
'CAUSE EVERY DAY IS DIFFERENT THAN BEFORE.	
FORCED INTO UNDERSTANDING	AH HAH

LILLI.
> WE AREN'T KIDS ANYMORE.
>
> IF WE SIT IN THAT PLACE IN OUR HEAD FOR TOO LONG
> THE PREVIOUS VERSIONS OF YOU FOR TOO LONG,

LILLI.

	THE GROUP.
WHEN YOU DIDN'T MIND THAT THE DAYS	
FELT A LITTLE TOO LONG,	OO
OR FEELING INSANE FOR	
A LITTLE TOO LONG,	AH

LILLI.
> JUST TAKE A GLANCE, 'CAUSE I BELIEVE
> IF YOU STAY THERE LONG ENOUGH,
> YOU'LL NEVER WANNA LEAVE.
> WHY WOULD YOU EVER LEAVE?
>
> GO AHEAD, THINK ON BACK TO WHEN YOU WERE A KID.
> MEMORIZE EVERY LINE FROM EACH SCENE THAT YOU'RE IN.
> RECITE THEM WHENEVER YOU'RE SCARED

THE GROUP.
> AH

LILLI.
>WHEN LIFE SEEMS IN FLUX,

THE GROUP.
>AH

LILLI.
>WE'RE NEVER PREPARED FOR
>   HOW GROWING UP SUCKS

THE GROUP.
>AH

LILLI.
>NO MATTER THE CROSS WE TOW,
>EVERYBODY HAS TO GROW UP,
>
>AND JUST LIKE THAT, YOU FEEL LOST,
>TRYING TO FIGURE OUT JUST WHERE TO GO.
>WHAT CAN YOU DO WHEN YOU'RE TOSSED
>IN THE MIDDLE OF THIS SO-CALLED NORMAL
>WITH THE LITTLE YOU KNOW?

LILLI.
>NO MORE TIME FOR GAMES.
>AND EVERY DAY IS THE SAME JUST
>   AS BEFORE.
>CLOSER TO UNDERSTANDING

THE GROUP.
>AH
>
>
>AH HAH

LILLI.
>WE AREN'T KIDS ANYMORE.
>FORCED INTO UNDERSTANDING
>WE AREN'T KIDS ANYMORE.

>*(**THE GROUP** is seated. **NICK**, seated, takes a breath. **THE GROUP** looks to him.)*
>
>*(In his time...**NICK** starts to speak.)*

NICK. I wrote a note for my parents to see...

Saying that I wanted to cut my sleeves with some cutlery.

Not slash the avenues, but streak the streets. I wanted to bleed...out.

And I would never speak out, but on the inside I want to scream, shout for help.

There was a dark cloud hovering and I needed covering.

I heard others speak. Drummers beat in the summer heat, but it wasn't until I heard that sweet sound of your voice telling me to stick around that I found recovery.

You pulled my head out of the ground and gave me the shove I need to seek therapy and share my dreams… and nightmares. Realize that there's other people out there that are just as scared. And while life is not fair, having the courage to stare it in the face and dare to claim your space is like that snare played with the bass…music.

Listen. And you'll intuit all you need to get through it.

The beauty is all around you once you're on your path to pursue it.

You may think that you blew it, but you're just like me, and like Nike, we gotta just *do* it.

[MUSIC NO. 18 "I'LL STICK AROUND"]

LIKE A WHISPER,
I DON'T ECHO IN THE CANYON,
I JUST BURROW DEEP INSIDE OF ME.
RECONSIDER
EVERY LIGHT THAT I SEE FADING
AS AN OPEN INVITATION
TO EVERYWHERE I CHOOSE TO GO.

BUT YOU SAY NO,
WE DON'T LET SADNESS MOVE ALONG.
WE ALL SHOULD AIR OUR DIRTY LAUNDRY OUT
AND SEE HOW FAR IT GOES.
OH, NOTHING COMPARES TO BEING TRUTHFUL,
FEELING HOPE FOR ALL THE YOUTHFUL SOULS
WHO FEAR THEY'RE NEVER FOUND.

I'LL STICK AROUND.
I'LL STICK AROUND.
AS LONG AS BOTH MY FEET ARE ON THE GROUND,
I'LL STICK AROUND.

LIKE A PROMISE,
I'M A FLOATING BIT OF DUST,
A TINY BUBBLE ON THE CRUST OF CALIFORNIA,
AT THE SMALLEST...
THE BASE OF MOUNTAIN TAMALPAIS,
AT THE BOTTOM FROM THE HIGHEST...
SOMETIMES WHERE I WANNA STAY.
BUT YOU SAY

NICK & THE GROUP.
NO,

NICK.
WE DON'T LET SADNESS MOVE ALONG.
WE ALL SHOULD AIR OUR DIRTY LAUNDRY OUT
AND SEE HOW FAR IT GOES.

NICK & THE GROUP.
OH,

NICK.
NOTHING COMPARES TO BEING TRUTHFUL,
FEELING HOPE FOR ALL THE YOUTHFUL SOULS
WHO FEAR THEY'RE NEVER FOUND.

NICK.	**THE GROUP.**
I'LL STICK AROUND.	OUND OUND
I'LL STICK AROUND.	OUND OUND
AS LONG AS BOTH MY FEET ARE ON THE GROUND,	
I'LL STICK AROUND.	OUND OUND
I NEVER SAID I WAS A GOOD GUY	
OR THAT I EVER NEEDED CREDIT FOR THE GOOD TRIES.	

NICK.	**THE GROUP.**
IF SKY'S THE LIMIT,	OH
WHY'M I ALWAYS	
LOOKING AT THE GROUND?	OH WHOA
WITH THAT "COULDA, SHOULDA, WOULDA"	OH
KIND OF HINDSIGHT,	
I'M AT A CLEARING CALLED	OH
"THE END OF THE ROPE"	OH
AND I'M LOOKING UP FOR THE FIRST TIME EVER	OH
AND ALL I SEE IS HOPE.	
	OH OH OH OH OO.

(**BONNIE**, *in her own time, physically connects with* **NICK** *in a gesture of friendship.* **COLTON** *follows suit as the rest sing in support of* **NICK**.)

NICK.

STILL YOU SAY NO,
WE DON'T LET SADNESS MOVE ALONG.
WE ALL SHOULD AIR OUR DIRTY LAUNDRY OUT
AND SEE HOW FAR IT GOES.

NICK.	**THE GROUP.**
OH, NOTHING COMPARES	OH
TO BEING TRUTHFUL,	OO
FEELING HOPE FOR ALL THE	OO
YOUTHFUL SOULS,	AH
WHO FEAR THEY'RE NEVER FOUND.	OO OH
I'LL STICK AROUND.	OUND OUND
I'LL STICK AROUND.	OUND OUND
AS LONG AS BOTH MY FEET ARE ON THE GROUND,	
I'LL STICK AROUND.	OUND OUND
	OH OO

(Lights out on **THE GROUP**: *Seated. Relaxed. Connected to each other.)*

(Blackout.)

[MUSIC NO. 19 "WHEN I GO"]

(Lights up on:)

COLTON.
I'LL HIT THE WALL AND I WON'T EVEN KNOW IT
TILL YOU PEEL MY BODY OFF THE BRICKS.
I TRY TO BREATH, MY LUNGS CAN'T EVEN HOLD IT IN,

COLTON.	**THE GROUP.**
I EXHALE.	AH

COLTON.
TEN YEARS OF FEARING EVERY TURN I WAS TAKING,
EVEN WHILE PRETENDING NOT TO BE.
I CUT THE VEIN AND HOPE THAT YOU SEE IT BLEED,

COLTON.	**THE GROUP.**
OH, I EXHALE.	AH
I CAN'T FAIL.	OO

RAY.
I'M LIVIN' IN WHAT STARTED OUT LIKE A DREAM.
I'M WORKIN' FOR THE THINKERS ON THE SCENE.
I'M FIGHTIN' FOR THE CHANCE TO BE UNDEFINED.
I'M LEAVING SOMETHIN' BEHIND.

RAY & BONNIE.
I'M WAITIN' FOR THIS MESSY LIGHT TO TURN GREEN
I'M HOPIN' FOR

RAY.
THE CHANCE TO WIPE IT CLEAN.

RAY & BONNIE.

	THE GROUP.
I'M DYING FOR	
THE ONES WHO COME TO	THE ONES WHO COME
THE SHOW.	TO THE SHOW. OO.

RAY.
> I'M LEAVING SOMETHING
>   WHEN I GO. OH.
> ALL I KNOW,
> EVEN WHEN IT'S OVER
> I'M LEAVING SOMETHING
>   WHEN I GO.

THE GROUP.
> OO OH.
>
> OO OH.

LILLI.
> YOU JINGLE KEYS TO FIND THAT'S FAR FROM AN OPTION.
> YOU'RE SERVING BABIES FACES MADE OF STONE.
> YOU SCREAM THROUGH TEARS TO GET THE BABY TO
>   LAUGH, OH NO.
> JUST EXHALE.

NICK.
> PUSH THROUGH THE CITY,
> WEAR YOUR PAIN LIKE A JACKET,
> YOU WALK WITH GIANTS, BUT THEY'RE IN THE CLOUDS.
> SOMETIMES YOU STRETCH TO REACH THE TOP OF THE
>   STACK,
> OH, DON'T EXHALE.

THE GROUP.
> DON'T EXHALE.

NICK.
> CANNOT FAIL.

THE GROUP.
> CANNOT FAIL.

NICK.
> I'M LIVING IN WHAT STARTED OUT LIKE A DREAM.
> I'M WORKING FOR THE THINKERS ON THE SCENE.
> I'M FIGHTING FOR THE CHANCE TO BE UNDEFINED.

THE GROUP.
> AH

NICK.
> I'M LEAVING SOMETHING BEHIND.

NICK & THE GROUP.
> I'M WAITING FOR THIS MESSY LIGHT TO TURN GREEN.
> I'M HOPING FOR THE CHANCE TO WIPE IT CLEAN.
> I'M DYING FOR THE ONES WHO COME TO THE SHOW OO.

NICK.	**THE GROUP.**
I'M LEAVING SOMETHING WHEN I GO, OH.	OH OH OH OH.
ALL I KNOW,	ALL I KNOW.
EVEN WHEN IT'S OVER	OO.
I'M LEAVING SOMETHING WHEN I GO.	OO OH.

COLTON.
> ALL THAT I HOPE FOR
> IS ALL THAT I QUESTION.
> IS THERE A RHYME OR A REASON
> OR A METHOD TO THE MADNESS?

COLTON.	**THE GROUP.**
I'M OPEN TO SUGGESTIONS.	OO.

LILLI.
> REMEMBER THAT IT'S REAL,
> THE NEED TO CREATE IT.
> THE VERY THING THAT FULFILLS YOU.

COLTON & LILLI.
> WATER'S FINE, JUMP INSIDE.
> SOMETIMES THE VERY THING YOU LIVE FOR
> IS THE THING THAT CAN KILL YOU.

COLTON.
> WATER'S FINE, JUMP INSIDE.
> SOMETIMES THE VERY THING YOU LIVE FOR
> IS THE THING THAT CAN KILL YOU.

BONNIE.
>SOMETIMES I'M STANDING WHERE THE NOOSE SHOULD BE HANGING.
>SOMETIMES A LEGACY GETS TIED IN KNOTS.
>SWING FROM THE RAFTERS, WATCH THE ARTIST, HE'S DANGLING,

BONNIE.	**THE GROUP.**
OH. CAN'T EXHALE.	AH.
FLY OR FAIL.	
	FLY OR FAIL.

RAY.
>I'M LIVING IN WHAT STARTED OUT LIKE A DREAM.
>I'M WORKING FOR THE THINKERS ON THE SCENE.
>I'M FIGHTING FOR THE CHANCE TO BE UNDEFINED.

THE GROUP.
>AH

RAY.
>I'M LEAVING SOMETHING BEHIND.

BONNIE & THE GROUP.
>I'M WAITING FOR THIS MESSY LIGHT TO TURN GREEN.
>I'M HOPING FOR THE CHANCE TO WIPE IT CLEAN.
>I'M DYING FOR THE ONES WHO COME TO THE SHOW.

THE GROUP.
>OH.

BONNIE.	**THE GROUP.**
I'M LEAVING SOMETHING WHEN I GO, OH. AND	OH OH OH.
ALL I KNOW,	ALL I KNOW.
EVEN WHEN IT'S OVER –	OO AH.

COLTON.
>I'M LEAVING SOMETHING WHEN I GO.

THE GROUP.
>GO, OH

COLTON.
WHEN I GO.

THE GROUP.
GO, OH

COLTON.	**THE GROUP.**
WHEN I,	OH
I GO.	OH

THE GROUP.
WHEN I GO

(Blackout.)

The End